A B C

A is for Allie, the artist
B is for Ben, the writer
C is for Cat, the subject

P is for Pun, which rhymes with Fun

ALLIECATS

53 Graphic Tales & Fun Puns About Cats

ALLIECATS

53 Graphic Tales & Fun Puns About Cats

ALLIECATS
53 Graphic Tales & Fun Puns About Cats

words & text by
Ben Stoltzfus

illustrations by
Allie Kirschner

39 WEST PRESS

39 WEST PRESS
Kansas City, MO
www.39WestPress.com

Copyright © 2019 by Ben Stoltzfus & Allie Kirschner

All rights reserved. No part of this book may be reproduced, scanned, or distributed in any printed or electronic form, including information storage and retrieval systems, without permission. Please do not participate in or encourage piracy of copyrighted materials in violation of the author's rights. Please purchase only authorized editions.

First Edition: November 2019

ISBN: 978-1-946358-26-4

Library of Congress Control Number: 2019946320

10 9 8 7 6 5 4 3 2 1

Interior Illustrations: Allie Kirschner
Book Design: j.d.tulloch
Graphic Tales Font: Chinacat

39WP-29-P

For Cool Cats

Contents

Preface   xiii
Introduction   xvii

catalog   3
cataclysm   4
catalectic   5
catagmatic   6
catacorolla   7
catamenia   8
catenate   9
catercornered   10
catnap   11
catgut   12
catastrophe   13
cater-cousin   14
cat's paw   15
catadromous   16
caterer   17
cat's cradle   18
cat haw   19
catbird   20
catabatic   21
catmobile   22
catsup   23
catatonic   24
Catawba   25

catalepsy	26
catacoustics	27
cat pipe	28
catcalling	29
catnip	30
caterwaul	31
catasterism	32
catso	33
cat eyes	34
cathouse	35
cat-o'-nine-tails	36
catabaptist	37
catachresis	38
catapult	39
catafalque	40
catalysis	41
cataract	42
cataract	43
catacomb	44
cathead	45
catwalk	46
catodon	47
catfish	48
caterpillar	49
catadypsidae	50
cattail	51
catalo	52
katydid	53
kittywake	54
Catalina	55
Etymological Glossary	57
About the Author & Artist	59

"When I use a word," Humpty Dumpty said, in rather a scornful tone, "it means just what I choose it to mean—neither more nor less."

"The question is," said Alice, "whether you can make words mean so many different things."

> **–Lewis Carroll, *Through the Looking Glass***

Preface

Tourrettes-sur-Loup is a charming medieval French town set in the foothills of the Maritime Alps. Unlike its neighbor, Vence, it cannot claim Marc Chagall as a distinguished artist, the presence of D. H. Lawrence before he died, or the stained windows of the Matisse chapel. It does, however, have a commanding view of tiered olive groves, silver-green in the sunshine, and, in the distance, the blue Mediterranean. It also has cats. Cats of every color and stripe roam the narrow, cobblestone streets, claiming every alley, corner, and rooftop. They sleep on windowsills, in geranium flowerpots, and in the sunshine of the town square atop a Peugeot or a Citroen. They own Tourrettes. In the afternoon, they gather on one of the side streets, waiting to be fed. A little old lady opens a second-story window and, little by little, tosses, from a white bowl, scraps of meat, leftovers, and fish heads. Bunched in clusters of two or three, the cats eat.

In the late 1970s, while on a sabbatical leave from the University of California, I spent one year in Tourrettes with my wife Judith Palmer and three of our seven children: Sarah, Stephen, and Andrew. The kids attended the French school in Vence, Judith did rock paintings, and I did my writing. The town cats inspired my collection of short stories entitled *Cat O' Nine Tails*. The lead story, "Chapeau," is about a young woman who believes she is the reincarnation of Bastet, the Egyptian cat goddess. The woman also owns many chapeaux of different colors, and she puns on the word *chapeau*, which, in French, is composed of the prefix *cha(t)*, meaning cat, and the suffix *peau*, meaning skin. She also plays games with a cat-o'-nine-tails. Another story, "Heads or Tails," is actually set in Tourrettes. It is about a spouse who makes her husband capture and kill cats because their nighttime yowling interrupts her beauty sleep. All nine stories are about cats, and some of them detail the terrible things children and adults do to this beloved animal. The book is now out of print.

While in Tourrettes, I also ran across a book of cat cartoons based on composite words beginning with the prefix *chat*. Each illustration was that of a cat in relation to the word. The word *château* was accompanied by the image of Lord Cat in a chateau. The word *chatouiller* (to tickle) was illustrated by two cats tickling each other. The word *châtiment* (punishment) was illustrated by one cat whipping another one in a dungeon. The word *chateaubriand* was illustrated by a cat eating a porterhouse steak, and so on.

But the cats of Tourrettes lay dormant until late 2018 when I compiled, on a whim, eighty words beginning with the prefixes *cat-* and *cata-* and sent them to my granddaughter, Allie Kirschner, suggesting that she draw, in the spirit of the French *chat* book, cartoons based on the word-puns. She selected fifty-three of the word-puns and illustrated them with cats.

Then, on June 18, 2019, in a huge stroke of good luck, Stephen Herschler, the same Stephen who was with us in Tourrettes, happened to be reading his grandmother's journal. A 1911 entry, "All About the Cat," caught his eye.

Scan of original 1911 journal entry by Laurinne Palmer

The author, Laurinne Easter Palmer (née Mattern, 1897-1976), is Judith's mother, Stephen's grandmother, and Allie's great grandmother. Laurinne's middle name commemorates her birthday, Easter Sunday, April 18. She lived in Berkeley, California, and her journal entry was probably written during her first year of high school. It reveals an uncanny generational convergence of overlapping interest in cats and puns, which culminates in this playful collection, whose very title, *Alliecats*, is itself a pun, melding the words *Allie*, *alley*, and *cats* into a new associative framework of graphic tales. Like her great grandmother, Allie plays with the words *caterpillar*, *catfish*, *catbird*, *cataract*, and *catsup*, illustrating them with her images and humor.

Allie's drawing arm is also itself a pun because it has several tattoos that, together, denote one thing and connote something else. One tattoo says, "I live for the funk, I die for the funk," a phrase in a song by old school rap group Lords of the Underground and remixed later in a song by the Notorious B.I.G. The second tattoo is for the Wu-Tang Clan, another rap group that rose to prominence in the 1990s. These tattoos represent Allie's love of music, especially the funky styles of Biggie Smalls, James Brown, and Stevie Wonder. Listening to their music is, for her, a source of great happiness. Another tattoo is an image by Magritte entitled *The Lovers (Les Amants)*. It represents a man and a woman kissing, their heads covered in cloth. This image fulfills one of the requirements of surrealist art, that it be a source of disquiet.

The juxtaposition of these tattoos—two for happiness and one for disquiet—is a source of contradiction and, like puns, transforms one thing into something else. An alley cat is not an *Alliecat*. Or is it? Perhaps it is both. Perhaps, like happiness and disquiet, they coexist.

–Ben Stoltzfus
Riverside, California (June 2019)

Introduction

Have you ever wondered what a *cathead* is? You might expect it to be a head that looks like a cat. But is it? We are familiar with expressions such as "meathead" or "pinhead," but neither word means what the nouns denote. Generally speaking a meathead is slang for someone who is obtuse, and pinhead also refers to someone who may not be very bright. There is no meat on the former and no pin in the latter. And so it is for *cathead*, which is a nautical term referring to a strong beam projecting horizontally over a ship's bow. There is no cat or head, unless someone like Allie draws a beam with a cat's head on it in order to play with the idea and poke fun at the word by transforming it into a pun (see p. 45).

John Pollack wrote a book entitled *The Pun Also Rises*—a title that spoofs Ernest Hemingway's title, *The Sun Also Rises*. By changing the word "sun," to "pun" he is asking us to keep in mind two simultaneous ideas: one based on a sunrise—an all too familiar occurrence—and the second on "punrise," which does not exist, except in the writer's imagination. It is an apt title, nonetheless, because Pollack not only goes on to give witty examples of punning, he also defines what the pun is while writing an entertaining history of its use in the English language. Did you know that there are punning contests in which participants try to outpun each other in a contest of wits on a given topic?

A pun transforms one word or thing into another by changing the sound and meaning or, in the case of visual puns, relating them through sight. The image of a cat's head on a ship's prow transforms its horizontal beam, visually, into a pun because by playing with the meaning of words *and* images that are intrinsically connected by etymology or function, the images in *Alliecats* transform one thing into another. In *Upon a Pun* Paul Hammond and Patrick Hughes give the following example: "The excitement at the circus is in tents."

A listener is likely to hear one of two meanings, "in tents," or perhaps "intense." This is a homophonic pun, one that is based on homophones—words that sound alike but have different meanings. The difference is based entirely on sound and spelling. A slightly different example is based on wordplay. A prison architect once said that his walls were not built to scale. The word "scale" means "built according to certain proportions," but it also suggests that a prisoner trying to escape would have difficulty "scaling" such a wall. In this case, the alternating meanings of "scale" come from the Latin *scala*, meaning "ladder." Are the fifty-three word-images in this book arranged according to scale? Let's find out.

I have grouped them into sequences that tell stories—stories that go from *catalog* to *cat's paw*; from *catadromous* to *catalepsy*; from *catacoustics* to *cat-o'-nine-tails*; from *catabaptist* to *catacomb*; and from *cathead* to *Catalina*—fifty-three composite words and images that begin with the prefix *cat-* or *cata-*, which means "down," "against," and "back." It occurs in words originating from the Greek but is used also in modern English words formed after the Greek type, as in *catadromous*, meaning fish going down a river to the sea in order to spawn. That said, the caption for the cat image on the front cover is *catalog*. What is a catalogue?

As a noun the dictionary defines *catalog(ue)* as "a list, usually in alphabetical order, with brief notes on the names, articles, etc., listed." It may also be "a record of the books and other resources of a library" or "any list or register." As a verb we use the statement in order "to make a catalogue of" or "enter in a catalog." In library science the word describes the bibliographical and technical features of a publication. It comes from the Latin word *catalogus* and the Greek word *catálogos*, meaning "list." I, for one, am old enough to remember the Sears, Roebuck and Co. catalogue from which American farmers and their wives could order tools, clothes, and household items. Today, Amazon's Internet catalogue is where everybody buys every item imaginable. Enough said, however, about catalog(ue) as an object and verb, or the meaning of *cata-* as a prefix. Let us scale the wall, escape from etymology, and, if this preamble has been too scholarly, try to have some fun.

My uncle's farm in upstate New York was where, as a kid, I first discovered the Sears, Roebuck catalogue. I was sitting in the outhouse, and there it was, so I leafed through it, looking at the pictures and the prices of the items listed. When I was finished I tore out a page and used it. Now, decades later,

I realize that I had transformed that page into something else. We could even say that the page also served; and this service of the page becomes a pun in its own right. But, in addition to being a page in a book, a page is also a boy servant, a youth in attendance on a person of rank. When I say, "The page also serves," do you see me in the outhouse or do you see the king's page bringing him a flagon of wine? Either description will do, and the point is that our understanding of it oscillates between the two, as it did for the architect's "not to scale" drawing for the wall.

If a catalog is defined as a long list of items, a captain's log is the record of daily events at sea. At the end of the voyage we can read his lists. Suppose, however, that the hull of the sailboat hits a submerged rock and the ship begins to list. This is a list of another kind and, as the ship limps into port, it lists. These lists are doing double duty. Fortunately, this will be my last maritime detail. So, let's leave the captain's log where it is and return to this book's cover and the cat on a log.

The word *catalog*, as defined, also does double duty: it is both object and activity, and it is a pun. As a pun, the prefix *cata-* is followed by the suffix *log*. The image on the cover is that of a cat, a log, and a list—three noun-things—and, in our minds, we register the fact that the cat is engaged in making a list. It is making a list while also sitting on a log; and, in this case, a log is the trunk of a felled tree, not a captain's log. All in all this cat-on-a-log is asking us to juggle four concepts simultaneously: a) three nouns (cat, log, and list); b) two verbs (to make a list and to sit); c) to focus on the verbal play and the meaning of words; and d) to visualize the combination of the animal, the objects, and the activities associated with them as they are transformed into something else. But there is more. The image itself is funny, and the humor associated with it not only makes us chuckle, it also shows us that playing with words and images is akin to playing with ideas. Puns are therefore not mere linguistic coincidences, they also unveil a hidden connection between mind and object. We might even say that puns trace a path from a word or image to the world at large. René Magritte's caption for a pipe he had painted—"This is not a pipe" ("*Ceci n'est pas une pipe*")—is a humorous statement about an important philosophical concept, that is, words and images are not the things they represent. They allow us to talk about the world, but they themselves are not the world. In this respect we too can say that the image on the cover of this book "is not a cat-on-a-log making a list." These words and images are only signifiers. They are guides to the world around us, but they themselves are not the things to which they refer. Philosophical issues notwithstanding, let us return to the pun and see how it works.

Puns as words occupy that happy ground where sound and sense collide. Visual puns add an extra dimension to the process where similarities of spelling, pronunciation, and image meet above ambiguous seams of meaning. Many people think that puns are the lowest form of humor, whereas, in fact, they display a high degree of wit and insight. Sigmund Freud believed that puns, like dreams, are the result of "displacement" and "compression." This means that the word and the image are not always what they seem to be. They denote one thing but connote something else, and when combined the two together form new meanings. Freud coined the neologism "alcoholidays" in order to describe human activity at certain times of the year. The word is a pun, and it combines two words, "alcohol" and "holidays," compressed into one. The two words are not necessarily related, but when displaced from their normal function and combined, they amuse us because we acknowledge the fact that drinking and holidays do frequently go together. Linguistically they are held together by the letters "hol," letters that belong to the ending of one word and the beginning of another.

Puns enable us to hold in mind simultaneously two or more different ideas about the same thing. For example the caption and image for *catatonic* (see p. 24), like *catalog*, allow us to play with multiple concepts: there is the prefix *cata-* followed by the suffix *tonic;* both words are embedded in the master-word *catatonic*, a psychiatric term most frequently used in schizophrenia where the subject displays muscular rigidity and mental stupor sometimes alternating with great excitement and confusion. Allie's image and caption capture many of these symptoms. Also, when tonic water is added to gin we have a drink known as a "gin and tonic." Her cat displays many signs of inebriation associated with muscular dysfunction and mental stupor. The bottles, labels, and confusion on the cat's face confirm the diagnosis.

Puns fold words, knowledge, and images into ideas—ideas that ask us to grasp two or three things at once. In the case of *catatonic* we have a triple pun: the cat, the tonic, and the state of confusion that results from imbibing too much. As these images and words play back and forth we acknowledge their truthfulness, visually, and acoustically. Most of all, their wit amuses us by showing how the names for things intertwine with the things themselves. In poems, words may rhyme; in puns, ideas rhyme, and, after transforming one thing into another, or one idea into another, they keep the reader skipping back and forth between two or three meanings. Furthermore, through deft juxtapositions puns reveal unseen relations among things and people. Puns tend to reorder ordinary associations; new meanings emerge that are illuminating. They allow us to affirm alternative points of view about familiar subjects and situations.

Samuel Taylor Coleridge viewed punning as a poetic act. As such, punning is not only an exercise in intelligence, it also exhibits sensitivity to subtle, unconnected relationships. The word and image *catacoustics* is one example among many (see p. 27). *Catacoustics* is the science of acoustics that treats reflected sounds. In this case the artist has drawn the image of a cat playing a guitar. Once again we have the composite play on word, image, and sound. The cat and the musical notes from the guitar (sound) are reflected in the mirror opposite them, while the mirror, as a specular trope, like Magritte's pipe that is not a pipe, calls our attention to a creative act that engages the artist: playing music, drawing, and writing become acts that can be construed as poetic. In *catacoustics*, as in art, the reflected image in a mirror tends to subvert realism by emphasizing the creative process. Puns by their very nature are also subversive whether we like it or not. They undermine expectations and received ideas in favor of fresh associations. They reflect combinations that foreground new possibilities, new ideas, and new ways of thinking. Poetic acts such as these enable us to discover similarities in the dissimilar, thereby compelling us to accept two self-consistent yet incompatible frames of reference. As Freud demonstrated, the conscious and unconscious processes underlying dreams and creativity are essentially the same. By bringing together previously separate areas of knowledge and experience they become combinatorial activities. They give us fresh insights. The verbal and visual acrobatics of *Alliecats* thus exhibit a high degree of imagination and playfulness. The Greeks had a word for it: *paronomasia*, which means "pun," coming from *para-* ("beside") and *onomasia* ("to name"). Additional word-images such as *catnap, catbird, cat eyes, cathouse,* and *cataract,* like all the others, are puns naming new ideas, new possibilities, and new horizons of expectation.

–Ben Stoltzfus
Riverside, California (March 2019)

ALLIECATS
53 Graphic Tales & Fun Puns About Cats

catalog

a long list of something or other

cataclysm

an upheaval

catalectic

a line of verse that is
missing part of the last foot

catagmatic

promoting the union of fractured bones

catacorolla

an abnormal growth of
petals inside the corolla of a flower

catamenia

menstruation

catenate

to link

catercornered

at a diagonal

catnap

a short nap

catgut

intestine of sheep for
strings of musical instruments

catastrophe

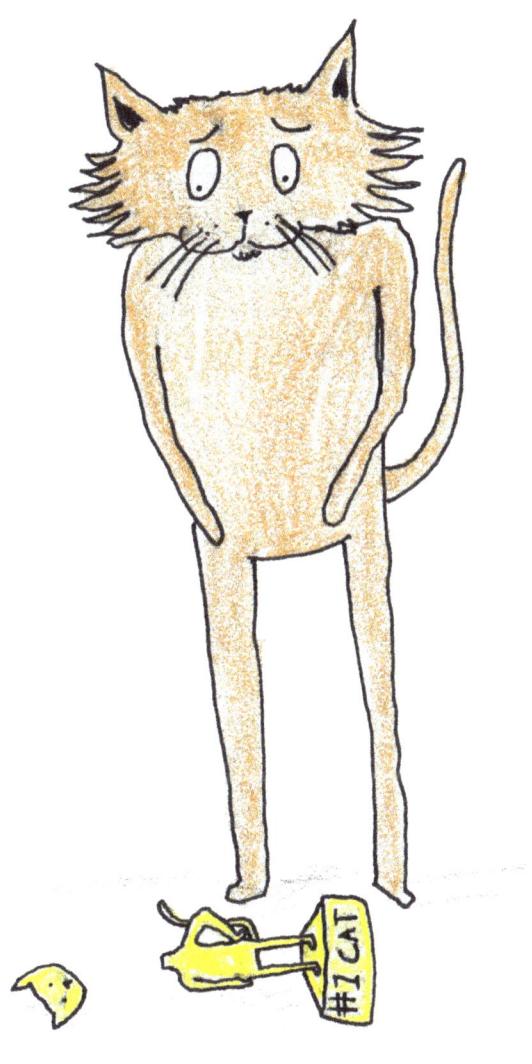

a calamity; a disaster

cater-cousin

an intimate friend

cat's paw

a person used by another; a tool

catadromous

many fish going down a river to spawn

caterer

a person who provides food and services for parties

cat's cradle

a game of strings for two children

cat haw

the berry of the hawthorn

catbird

has the call like the mewing of a cat

catabatic

to go down slowly; yielding

catmobile

the vehicle driven by a cat

catsup

variant spelling of ketchup

catatonic

a person who exhibits a condition
of rigidity as though frozen in space

Catawba

a wine made from the
reddish grape of the same name

catalepsy

muscular rigidity; fixity of posture

catacoustics

the science of acoustics
that treats reflected sounds

catpipe

a pipe for making catcalls

catcalling

to whistle, shout, or make a comment
of a sexual nature to a woman passing by

catnip

a plant of the mint family that appeals to cats

caterwaul

to cry as cats do during rutting

catasterism

to place among the stars

catso

a cheat; a rogue

cat eyes

rolling "snake eyes" with a pair of dice

cathouse

a house of prostitution

cat-o'-nine-tails

a whip with nine knotted lines

catabaptist

someone who opposes baptism

catachresis

the misuse of a word

catapult

a medieval weapon that projects rocks

catafalque

a raised platform for the dead

catalysis

dissolution; decay

cataract

a clouding of the lens of the
eye that results in blurred vision

cataract

a large waterfall

catacomb

a grotto; a tomb in the ground

cathead

a strong beam projecting
horizontally over a ship's bow

catwalk

a narrow plank used as a walkway

catodon

a sperm whale with teeth only in the lower jaw

catfish

a freshwater or marine fish, typically bottom dwelling, with whisker-like barbels around the mouth

caterpillar

the worm-like, often hairy
larvae of lepidopterous insects

catadypsidae

a North-American spider with vertical fangs

cattail

a tall, reed-like marsh plant

catalo

a cross between a bison and a cow

katydid

a large, green tree insect
related to the grasshopper

kittywake

a three-toed seagull

Catalina

an island off the coast of Southern California

Etymological Glossary
Selected Words

cat: Old English *catt*; German *Katze*; French *chat*
catachresis: Greek *katakhrēsis* (misuse)
cataclysm: Greek *kataklysmós* (deluge)
catacomb: Latin *catacumbās*; Old English *catacumbe*
catafalque: French *catafalque*; Italian *catafalco*
catalectic: Greek *katalēktikós* (incomplete)
catalepsy: Greek *katálēpsis* (seizure)
catalogue: Greek *katálogos*
catamenia: Greek *katamēnia*
catapult: Greek *katapéltēs*
cataract: Greek *katarráktēs* (downrushing)
catastrophe: Greek *katastrophē* (overturning)
Catawba: Siouan *kátapu* (fork of a stream)
caterpillar: Latin *catta pilosa* (hairy cat)
caterwaul: Middle English *cater(wawen)* (*cater* tomcat + *wawen* to howl)

About the Author & Artist

Ben Stoltzfus is Professor Emeritus of Comparative Literature and Creative Writing at the University of California, Riverside. He has published novels, essays, and books of literary criticism. His most recent novel, *Dumpster, for God's Sake*, is a parody of Loviers City, a town whose motto is "Cleanliness Is Next to Godliness." The sanitary squadrons are well on their way to achieving Godliness when a miraculous sighting of the Virgin disrupts the town's endeavors. Tourists, undocumented immigrants, cultists, and the faithful flock to Loviers City, where, unaware of the town's motto, they discard their trash, littering the streets and the walnut groves. The garbage trucks cannot keep up. The Virgin triumphs. Stoltzfus lives in Riverside, California with his artist wife, Judith Palmer. Allie Kirschner is their granddaughter.

Allie Kirschner has enjoyed drawing ever since she can remember. She honed her skills as a visual arts major at Pioneer Valley Performing Arts Charter School. Allie matriculated to Greenfield Community College, where she studies visual arts. She lives in Northampton, Massachusetts, with her cat Maizy.

www.ingramcontent.com/pod-product-compliance
Lightning Source LLC
Chambersburg PA
CBHW040124130526
44591CB00041B/2993